"I have heard their groans and sighs, and seen their tears, and I would give every drop of blood in my veins to free them."

—HARRIET TUBMAN

$100 REWARD!

RANAWAY

From the undersigned, living on Current River, about twelve miles above Doniphan, in Ripley County, Mo., on 3nd of March, 1860, **A NEGRO MAN**, about 30 years old, weighs about 160 pounds; high forehead, with a scar on it; had on brown pants and coat very much worn, and an old black wool hat; shoes size No. 11.

The above reward will be given to any person who may apprehend this said negro out of the State; and fifty dollars if apprehended in this State outside of Ripley county, or $25 if taken in Ripley county.

APOS TUCKER.

THE UNDERGROUND RAILROAD

BY CARLA WILLIAMS

The Child's World

COVER PHOTO

Harriet Tubman (far left) with slaves she helped escape to freedom on the Underground Railroad
©Corbis-Bettmann

Published in the United States of America by The Child's World®, Inc.
PO Box 326
Chanhassen, MN 55317-0326
800-599-READ
www.childsworld.com

Product Manager Mary Francis-DeMarois/The Creative Spark
Designer Robert E. Bonaker/Graphic Design & Consulting Co.
Editorial Direction Elizabeth Sirimarco Budd
Contributors Mary Berendes, Red Line Editorial, Katherine Stevenson, Ph.D.

Library of Congress Cataloging-in-Publication Data
Williams, Carla, 1965–
The Underground Railroad / by Carla Williams.
p. cm.
Includes bibliographical references and index.
ISBN 1-56766-926-3 (lib. bdg. : alk. paper)
1. Underground railroad—Juvenile literature. 2. Fugitive
slaves—United States—History—19th century—Juvenile literature.
[1. Underground railroad. 2. Fugitive slaves.]   I. Title.
E450 .W7 2001
973.7'115—dc21
                    2001001076

Contents

Slavery and Abolition

The Underground Railroad wasn't a railroad, and it wasn't underground. So what was it? The Underground Railroad was a network of people in the United States who helped black people escape during the time of slavery.

Years ago, people from many different parts of Africa were taken from their homelands. They were taken by force and **enslaved.** Slave traders brought them to America and to other lands. The first enslaved Africans arrived in America in 1619. Slavery in America would last for about 240 years—longer than the United States has been a country.

Slaves were brought across the Atlantic Ocean on large ships. They lay in dark, cramped spaces in the bottoms of the ships, chained together and forced to lie naked on wooden planks. They were not allowed to stand up or even to go to the bathroom. Those who became ill were thrown into the ocean to drown.

It is estimated that about 1.8 million African slaves died during these difficult journeys across the Atlantic.

When the African slaves got off the ships, they were taken to a public **auction** and sold to the highest bidder. They were separated from their families. Most never saw their loved ones again. Usually slaves were sent to work in the Southern states. They worked on plantations, large farms owned by white people. Some worked in cities rather than in the country. The Northern states had fewer farms and many fewer slaves. Over time, the Northern states outlawed slavery.

Slaves were forced to work long hours for no pay. They were bought and sold like animals. They were not even considered to be human beings, and they had no rights. Slave masters beat and sometimes killed their slaves. The slave masters were not punished for such treatment because it was not against the law.

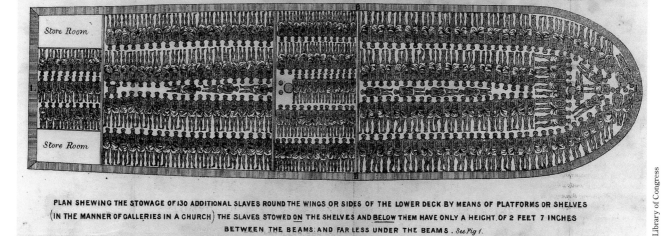

PLAN OF LOWER DECK WITH THE STOWAGE OF 292 SLAVES

130 OF THESE BEING STOWED UNDER THE SHELVES AS SHEWN IN FIGURE D & FIGURE 5.

Store Room

Store Room

PLAN SHEWING THE STOWAGE OF 130 ADDITIONAL SLAVES ROUND THE WINGS OR SIDES OF THE LOWER DECK BY MEANS OF PLATFORMS OR SHELVES (IN THE MANNER OF GALLERIES IN A CHURCH) THE SLAVES STOWED ON THE SHELVES AND BELOW THEM HAVE ONLY A HEIGHT OF 2 FEET 7 INCHES BETWEEN THE BEAMS; AND FAR LESS UNDER THE BEAMS. See Fig 1.

THE DRAWING ABOVE SHOWS A PLAN FOR SLAVE QUARTERS ON A SHIP. AFRICANS WERE TRANSPORTED TO SLAVERY UNDER TERRIBLE CONDITIONS. THEY WERE CROWDED ONTO SHIPS AND FORCED UNDER THE DECK INTO DARK, DIRTY, HOT SPACES. OVER THE YEARS, AN ESTIMATED 1.8 MILLION SLAVES DIED DURING THE VOYAGE ACROSS THE ATLANTIC.

North Wind Pictures

WHEN SLAVES WERE SOLD AT AUCTION, THEY WERE OFTEN SEPARATED FROM THEIR FAMILIES, NEVER TO SEE EACH OTHER AGAIN.

Many slaves tried to escape from their owners. For a while, escaped slaves who reached the free states in the North were no longer slaves. But the slave owners did not want slaves to be able to gain their freedom. Instead, they wanted to keep these workers on their plantations and farms. A law called the **Fugitive** Slave Act of 1850 made it illegal for slaves to escape. Under this law, escaped slaves had to be captured and returned to their owners. Even if the slaves reached the Northern states, they were not safe. They still could be captured and sent back to their owners. When they were sent back, they were usually punished severely. Despite the dangers, many slaves still tried to escape. They believed that it was better to seek freedom than to stay in a life of slavery. They did not want to be slaves. It was a terrible way to live.

The Fugitive Slave Act also made it a crime to help slaves escape. People who wanted to end slavery were called **abolitionists.** Most abolitionists were white people who lived in the North.

They believed that slavery was wrong and fought to change the laws that permitted it. Often they tried to help slaves escape. If the abolitionists were caught doing this, they could be punished, too.

Not every black person in the United States was a slave. There were also free black people, most of them living in the North and the West. Black people could become free in several different ways. Sometimes abolitionists bought slaves to set them free. Sometimes kind slave owners freed their own slaves. Other slaves escaped from owners who had brought them to the North. Sometimes free blacks bought freedom for other family members. And some people were free blacks who had never been enslaved. They had arrived on boats that landed in the North instead of the South. Free blacks carried special papers that kept other people from calling them slaves and taking them to the South. Many free black people were also abolitionists. They wanted to end the suffering of slavery.

The Burns Archive

IN 1800, MORE THAN 1 MILLION PEOPLE IN THE UNITED STATES—MEN, WOMEN, AND CHILDREN OF ALL AGES—WERE SLAVES. BY 1860, THAT NUMBER HAD INCREASED TO 4 MILLION. ALTHOUGH ESCAPING WAS DIFFICULT AND DANGEROUS, MANY SLAVES BELIEVED IT WAS WORTH RISKING THEIR LIVES TO REACH FREEDOM.

bolitionists and free blacks wanted to help slaves escape. They knew the slaves would have to escape in secret because the slave owners would try to stop them. The abolitionists and free blacks developed a system of safe houses, trails, and secret codes for slaves to follow. This system became known as the Underground Railroad.

Setting up and maintaining the Underground Railroad was far from easy. Communication was difficult. There were no telephones. Slaves were not allowed to learn how to read or write. Some slaves learned in secret, but most could not read even a simple message. They were rarely allowed to visit other slaves on different plantations.

North Wind Pictures

HISTORIANS ESTIMATE THAT ABOUT 1,000 SLAVES EACH YEAR ESCAPED TO FREEDOM ON THE UNDERGROUND RAILROAD. BUT FOR EVERY ONE WHO SUCCEEDED, MANY MORE TRIED AND FAILED. WHEN SLAVES LIKE THE TWO MEN SHOWN ABOVE WERE CAPTURED AND RETURNED TO THEIR MASTERS, THEY WERE USUALLY PUNISHED SEVERELY.

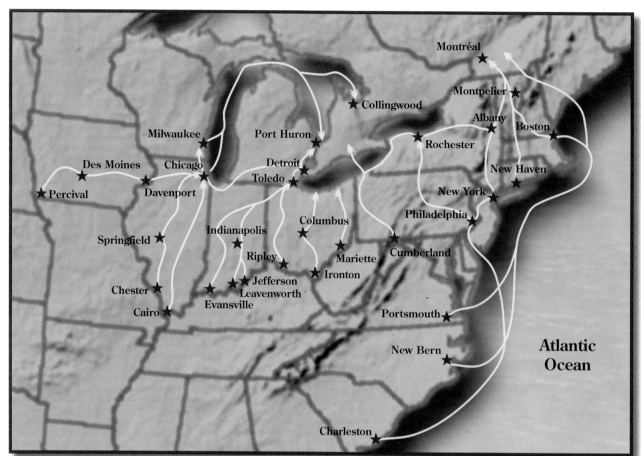

Robert Bonaker

THE MAP ABOVE SHOWS ROUTES OF THE UNDERGROUND RAILROAD.

Slaves could not hold meetings. Most were not permitted to go into town. Escape information had to come to them in secret or in code. All of the information about the Underground Railroad traveled by word of mouth. The Railroad workers were very clever. Sometimes they helped slaves escape using clues left in plain sight. Because the clues were in secret codes, the slave owners could not understand them.

When did people begin using the phrase "Underground Railroad?" One night, a slave named Tice Davids escaped from Kentucky. To get to the free state of Ohio, he had to swim across the Ohio River. When he got to the other side, he disappeared. His owner got in a boat and looked for Tice but never saw him again. The owner told his friends that Tice "must have gone off on an underground railroad." Later, a reporter said that a captured slave talked about a "railroad that went underground all the way to Boston." The name "Underground Railroad" comes from these stories. "Underground" meant that it was secret. "Railroad" meant that it was a way to travel from one point to another—from slavery to freedom.

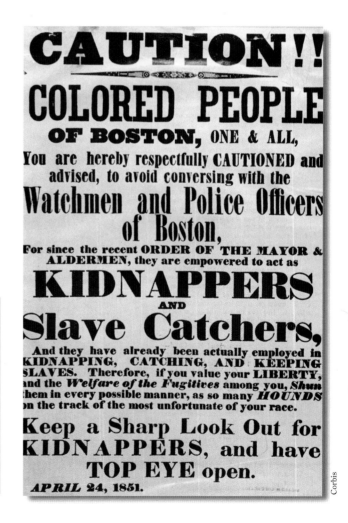

THIS POSTER WARNS BLACK RESIDENTS OF BOSTON TO BEWARE OF SLAVE CATCHERS. AFTER THE FUGITIVE SLAVE ACT WAS PASSED, EVEN FREE BLACKS WERE IN DANGER OF BEING CAPTURED AND SENT TO THE SOUTH —AND TO A LIFE OF SLAVERY.

MANY SLAVES FEARED WHAT WOULD BECOME OF THEM IF THEY ESCAPED. MOST HAD LITTLE OR NO EDUCATION AND KNEW NOTHING ABOUT LIFE BEYOND THE PLANTATIONS WHERE THEY LIVED AND WORKED. ESCAPING TO FREEDOM WAS FRIGHTENING AND RISKY.

Agents, Station Masters, and Conductors

Many slaves who escaped were not from plantations, but from Southern cities. These city slaves had received at least some education. Many could read and write. Some had even been able to save a little money. Their skills and their savings helped them survive after they escaped. They needed to be able to take care of themselves and earn a living once they were free. That is why slave owners tried to keep slaves from learning. They did not want the slaves to have the skills they needed to survive on their own.

Many slaves were afraid to try to escape. They knew nothing about the North. Most of them had never been allowed to leave their plantations. They could not be sure that they would find a better life in the North. More men tried to escape than women. Many women did not want to leave family members behind—especially their children.

Workers on the Underground Railroad were skilled at hiding the slaves and getting them to freedom. Thousands of people worked on the Railroad. Some gave abolitionist groups money to buy food and clothing for the escaped slaves. Other Railroad workers went South to guide the slaves to the North. Some opened their homes to fugitive slaves. This was very dangerous. If they were caught hiding slaves, they would be punished.

Most people who worked on the Railroad were not famous. Today no one even knows their names. But these people worked hard and were very brave. They gave themselves titles used by workers on real railroads. Each person had a different job to do. *Agents* helped people escape by giving them clues, money, or other help. *Stationmasters* took escaped slaves into their homes, or "stations," to hide them. *Conductors* guided people on the journeys. Some Underground Railroad workers became well known.

Harriet Tubman was born into slavery in Maryland. She worked as a field hand. When she was a child, her master often beat her. But Harriet was strong. One day, young Harriet tried to protect another slave from the **overseer** who watched over the slaves. The overseer hit Harriet in the head with a two-pound brass weight. For the rest of her life, she had a deep scar on her forehead and often had painful headaches. Her injury also caused her to black out without notice, but this never slowed her down.

North Wind Pictures

NO ONE KNOWS EXACTLY HOW MANY SLAVES ESCAPED DURING THE YEARS OF SLAVERY IN THE UNITED STATES. SOME ESTIMATES SUGGEST ABOUT 100,000 PEOPLE MADE THEIR WAY TO FREEDOM. ESCAPING TOOK A GREAT DEAL OF COURAGE. FUGITIVES LIKE THE MEN SHOWN ABOVE KNEW THEY COULD BE CAPTURED AT ANY TIME.

In 1849, Harriet found out that she and her brothers were going to be sold. She decided to escape. Her brothers and her husband John were afraid to try escaping, but Harriet was not. At about 28 years of age, she walked by herself from Maryland to Pennsylvania. Yet even though she was free, Harriet was not happy. She missed her family. Harriet decided that they should all be free with her. She would work in the North and save her pay. Then she would use the money to go back and get her family. First Harriet freed her sister and her sister's children. Then she went back and helped one brother and two other men escape. When she went back for her husband, he was afraid to come. She left him behind.

Harriet went back to the South 19 times. She helped more than 300 people escape. She helped most of her family to freedom, including her aged parents, her brothers and sisters, and their families. Like many escaped slaves, they all went to Canada. Because of the Fugitive Slave Act, the Northern states were not completely safe. But since Canada was another country, the same law did not apply there. Canada was the safest place to go.

Corbis

HARRIET TUBMAN (ABOVE) IS SAID TO HAVE HELPED MORE THAN 300 SLAVES ESCAPE TO FREEDOM. AFTER ESCAPING HERSELF, SHE RETURNED TO THE SOUTH 19 TIMES TO HELP OTHERS.

Harriet was very tough. She would not let anyone slow her down. In fact, she carried a gun—not to protect herself, but to force the fugitives to keep moving forward. If people she was helping tried to turn back, she threatened to shoot them. She knew that anyone who turned back could tell **bounty hunters** where to find her and the other fugitives. They might even reveal secrets about the Underground Railroad. She also felt strongly that nothing was worse than slavery. Despite her threats, Harriet never had to shoot anyone. And no one she helped ever went back to slavery.

Harriet was a conductor on the Underground Railroad. She was famous in her time. Slave owners offered large rewards for her capture. Even with the big scar on her head, Harriet was never recognized. Sometimes she fainted while she was helping people escape, but she was never captured. She saved so many people from slavery that she was called the "Moses of Her People." Like the man in the Bible, she led the former slaves to the "Promised Land" of freedom.

Frederick Douglass was another slave born in Maryland. His owner allowed him to work for other people and to keep part of the pay. Frederick did not spend any of his hard-earned money. He saved every penny so that one day he could escape. Frederick had a friend who was a free black man. He borrowed his friend's free papers. If Frederick was caught, he could use them to pretend that he was already free. In 1838, he escaped to Massachusetts. There he met and worked with abolitionists.

Frederick had a deep, beautiful voice. He became a famous speaker. He even traveled to England to speak against slavery. He published the story of his life so that people would know how terrible it was to be a slave. Frederick settled in Rochester, New York. There he published a newspaper about the abolitionist movement called the *North Star.* He later changed the name to *Frederick Douglass' Paper.* Rochester is also very close to the U.S. border with Canada. Frederick became an Underground Railroad stationmaster. His home was a station on the Railroad.

Frederick and his wife, Anna Murray Douglass, helped hundreds of escaped slaves reach Canada. But he reached many more people through his speeches and his writing.

Some of the people who worked on the Underground Railroad had never been slaves. Levi Coffin was a white man born in the Southern state of North Carolina. He believed from a young age that slavery was wrong.

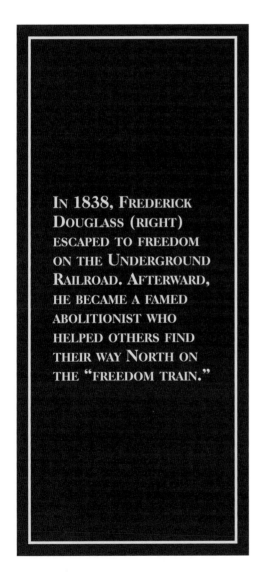

IN 1838, FREDERICK DOUGLASS (RIGHT) ESCAPED TO FREEDOM ON THE UNDERGROUND RAILROAD. AFTERWARD, HE BECAME A FAMED ABOLITIONIST WHO HELPED OTHERS FIND THEIR WAY NORTH ON THE "FREEDOM TRAIN."

Courtesy of the Levi Coffin House Association

When Levi was a boy, he and his father were walking one day and saw some slaves chained together. His father asked the slaves why they were chained. They said it was so they could not return to their families. Another time, a slave was beaten just for talking to Levi's father. Levi could not forget these things.

Later in life, Levi and his wife, Catharine, moved to Newport, Indiana. There they became abolitionists. Their house was known as "Grand Central Station" on the Underground Railroad. The Coffins later moved to Ohio, but they continued to help escaped slaves. Levi helped more than 3,000 people escape to freedom in Indiana and Ohio. Not one slave who stayed with the Coffins was captured or went back to slavery. Because of this, Levi was called the president of the Underground Railroad.

LEVI COFFIN (ABOVE) AND HIS WIFE, CATHARINE, HELPED MORE THAN 3,000 SLAVES TO FREEDOM. NO SLAVE WHO STAYED WITH THE COFFINS WAS EVER CAPTURED.

Courtesy of the Levi Coffin House Association

LEVI COFFIN'S EIGHT-ROOM BRICK HOUSE WAS KNOWN AS THE "GRAND CENTRAL STATION" OF THE UNDERGROUND RAILROAD. THOUSANDS OF BLACKS FLEEING TO FREEDOM STAYED IN THE HOME.

Creative Escapes

Most slaves escaped by walking to freedom. They traveled through the woods at night so they wouldn't be seen. To reach freedom, many slaves had to walk hundreds of miles. Sometimes their shoes wore out, and they had to walk barefoot the rest of the way. It was dark and scary in the woods. Bugs and snakes bit them. Sometimes they had to cross deep rivers and streams. They were cold, hungry, and tired. Their feet ached. Even so, they kept going. They knew that freedom lay ahead.

Some workers and slaves on the Underground Railroad found creative ways to help slaves escape. We know many of these stories today because of William Still. William was an African American who had been born free in Philadelphia, Pennsylvania. He went to work on the Underground Railroad. William could read and write. He kept daily records of Underground Railroad activity. Every day William wrote down the stories of the men and women who escaped through Philadelphia. He later published these stories so that other people would know them.

Many slave owners did not want their slaves to keep any of their old ways. They would not let them practice their own religions. They would not allow them to speak the languages of their African countries. But the owners let the slaves sing as they worked in the fields. That singing provided an idea for someone who wanted to help slaves escape.

Peg Leg Joe was an old white sailor. He worked as a handyman on different plantations. Joe's real reason for being in the South was to help slaves escape. He made up a song called "Follow the Drinking Gourd." The words to the song were clues to help slaves find their way to freedom. The escape route started at the Tombigbee River in Mobile, Alabama. The song told slaves to follow the path of the river.

WILLIAM STILL WAS A FREE BLACK WHO LIVED
IN PHILADELPHIA. HE HELPED MANY FUGITIVES
TO FREEDOM AND WROTE THE FIRST DETAILED
ACCOUNT OF THE UNDERGROUND RAILROAD.

Schomburg Center for Research in Black Culture

When the Sun comes back

And the first quail calls

Follow the Drinking Gourd.

For the old man is a-waiting for

  to carry you to freedom

If you follow the Drinking Gourd.

The riverbank makes a very good road.

The dead trees will show you the way.

Left foot, peg foot, traveling on,

Follow the Drinking Gourd.

The river ends between two hills

Follow the Drinking Gourd.

There's another river on the other side

Follow the Drinking Gourd.

When the great big river meets

  the little river

Follow the Drinking Gourd.

For the old man is a-waiting for

  to carry you to freedom

If you follow the Drinking Gourd.

The Drinking Gourd was the group of stars called the Big Dipper. The Big Dipper always points to the North Star. The North Star was a guide in the night sky. If escaping slaves followed the North Star, they would get to the North and to freedom. Whenever Peg Leg Joe went to work on a plantation, he would teach this song to the slaves. Then Joe would go through the woods and carve a picture of his peg leg on the tree trunks. Slaves would follow the North Star and the peg legs to safe houses and to freedom. Soon after Joe left a plantation, some of the slaves would escape. But no one suspected him of telling the slaves how to do it.

A HANDYMAN NAMED PEG LEG JOE TRAVELED FROM PLANTATION TO PLANTATION, TEACHING SLAVES A SONG THAT GAVE THEM INSTRUCTIONS TO FIND THEIR WAY TO FREEDOM. AT LEFT ARE THE LYRICS TO PEG LEG JOE'S SONG, "THE DRINKING GOURD." THE DRINKING GOURD WAS A CODE NAME FOR THE GROUP OF STARS CALLED THE BIG DIPPER.

Another clever set of clues was hidden in quilts. Slave women in the South made quilts for their families. Some women made up coded patterns for the quilts. Escaping slaves were able to read the codes within the quilts.

Information on the quilt code comes from Ozella McDaniel Williams. Her mother and grandmother passed the stories down to her. Much of what we know about the lives of slaves has come from **oral history.** Oral history is told in stories instead of written in books. According to Williams, 10 quilt patterns were part of the code. Each quilt contained one pattern. One by one, the quilts were hung out to dry or air out on a fence. Certain patterns in the quilts told escaping slaves what to do.

If a quilt showed a house with smoke coming out of the chimney, that meant that the house where the quilt hung was a safe house. A quilt with a wagon-wheel pattern meant that slaves should pack up everything that would fit in a wagon—it was time to go. A bear-paw pattern meant to follow fake bear-paw tracks through the woods. By reading the symbols on the quilts, many slaves were able to reach freedom. Bounty hunters sent to capture escaped slaves never knew the quilts were a code.

Courtesy of R. G. Dobard

OZELLA McDANIEL WILLIAMS (RIGHT) LEARNED ABOUT THE SECRET QUILT CODES FROM HER MOTHER AND GRANDMOTHER. MUCH OF WHAT WE KNOW ABOUT THE LIVES OF SLAVES HAS COME FROM ORAL HISTORIES, THE PASSING DOWN OF STORIES FROM GENERATION TO GENERATION.

Courtesy of R. G. Dobard

THE WAGON WHEEL PATTERN WAS ONE OF THE SECRET CODES HIDDEN IN QUILT PATTERNS.

Some slaves figured out their own ways to escape but still made use of the Underground Railroad. William and Ellen Craft were married slaves in Georgia. Ellen was a seamstress. She was very fair skinned and looked as if she were white. William was a cabinet-maker and a hotel waiter. He was very dark skinned. Ellen came up with a plan for their escape. She would pretend to be a white man. She asked William to buy her a man's suit. She wore high-heeled boots and a high hat to look taller. She wrapped her head in a handkerchief and claimed to have a toothache. The handkerchief kept people from seeing her face too closely and noticing that she had no whiskers. At the end of 1848, they made their escape.

William pretended to be Ellen's servant. Black servants often traveled with their white masters. No one thought it was strange. They were able to stay in nice hotels because the owners thought Ellen was white. Ellen could not read or write, so she wrapped her hand in a sling and pretended it was hurt. That way, she did not have to sign her name at the hotels. The Crafts went to Boston, but soon their old master found them. He sent bounty hunters to bring them back. The Crafts would not go back to slavery. Abolitionists helped them get out of town, and they settled in England, where slavery was illegal. Once slavery was outlawed in the United States, William and Ellen Craft returned. They bought a plantation and started a farm. They also opened a school.

Disguising herself as a boy brought another young woman to freedom. Anna Maria Weems was just 15 years old when she escaped from slavery in Washington, D.C. All of her family members had been sold. But Anna did not know that *abolitionists* had bought her family in order to set them free. Anna's owners would not sell her, however, so she figured out a clever way to escape. Anna knew that a girl traveling alone would attract attention. She also knew that if she ran away, her owners would report the escape of a young girl. So Anna dressed as a boy. No one noticed her, and she escaped to Philadelphia. Her owner offered a $500 reward for her capture, but she was not caught. From Philadelphia, Anna made it to New York. She later went to Canada, where she was able to go to school.

ELLEN CRAFT (LEFT) WAS SO LIGHT SKINNED THAT MANY PEOPLE
THOUGHT SHE WAS WHITE. SHE DRESSED AS A WHITE MAN (RIGHT)
TO ESCAPE WITH HER HUSBAND.

Several slaves mailed themselves to freedom in boxes. Henry Brown was a slave in Virginia who wanted to be free. In 1849, he decided to ship himself to Philadelphia. His friend Samuel Smith was a white carpenter. Henry ordered a box from Samuel. The box was big enough for Henry to fit inside. Henry brought a little water and a few biscuits. Smith addressed the box to abolitionist headquarters in Philadelphia. He marked it "This Side Up With Care." Not every postman set the box upright, and Henry spent much of the trip on his head. He was sometimes handled roughly. But after 26 hours in the box, he arrived safely in Philadelphia. He earned the nickname "Box" because of his clever escape. Henry "Box" Brown went to work for the Underground Railroad in Boston. Samuel Smith was later sent to prison for building crates for two other slaves.

Lear Green was a teenaged girl who used this same daring means of escape. Lear was a house servant in Baltimore. She had someone pack her into a sailor's chest. The chest was sent to Philadelphia on the same ship as her fiancé's mother. Lear ended up at the home of Underground Railroad worker William Still. He made sure she was safe until she arrived at her new home in New York.

FIFTEEN-YEAR-OLD ANNA MARIA WEEMS DRESSED AS A BOY TO ESCAPE SLAVERY.

AT THE START OF THE CIVIL WAR, MORE AFRICAN AMERICANS, LIKE THOSE SEEN HERE RIDING IN THE WAGON, BEGAN TO ESCAPE. MANY OF THEM JOINED UNION FORCES TO HELP THE NORTH WIN THE WAR. THEY HOPED THAT A NORTHERN VICTORY WOULD ONE DAY BRING FREEDOM FOR ALL.

And Freedom for All

Most black people who escaped on the Underground Railroad went to the free states of the North. Some went to Canada or Mexico. When the newly freed blacks reached freedom, they had to find jobs. They found out that not everyone in the North wanted to help black people. Some former slaves had a difficult time finding work in the North. Others did not know how to take care of themselves. As slaves, they never had to buy groceries or rent a room. Still, their new life in the North was far better than a life of slavery.

In 1861, the Northern states went to war with the South when the **Civil War** began. The **Union** army fought for the Northern states, and the **Confederate** army fought for the Southern states. One reason for the war was that the states could not agree on whether to make slavery illegal. Many Northerners thought that the South should free the slaves. Southerners refused and wanted to spread the system of slavery to new parts of the country.

Harriet Tubman and Frederick Douglass both worked for the Union army. Harriet was a nurse and a spy. Frederick's job was to encourage black men to join the Union army. Frederick was also a friend of President Abraham Lincoln. He often talked to Lincoln about **emancipation.**

Lincoln declared the Southern slaves free on January 1, 1863, when he signed the Emancipation Proclamation. But this law did not truly free the slaves, for the Confederate States no longer considered themselves part of the United States. They refused to accept a demand from the U.S. president. For two more years, war and slavery continued. Finally, in 1865, Confederate General Robert E. Lee **surrendered,** and the war soon ended. Later that year, slavery was made illegal by the 13th **Amendment** to the U.S. **Constitution.** There was no longer a need for the Underground Railroad.

THE EMANCIPATION PROCLAMATION OF 1863 DID
NOT TRULY FREE THE SLAVES, FOR SOUTHERN
SLAVE OWNERS REFUSED TO OBEY PRESIDENT
LINCOLN'S ORDERS. BUT TWO YEARS LATER,
THE 13TH AMENDMENT MADE SLAVERY ILLEGAL
THROUGHOUT THE UNITED STATES.

It has been almost 150 years since slaves in the United States were set free, but people still remember and honor the Underground Railroad. It is an important part of American history. Family stories, such as the quilt code, are handed down to keep the memory alive. Perhaps one of your ancestors worked on the Underground Railroad. Perhaps one of them escaped to freedom on it.

In 1990, the U.S. Congress asked the National Park Service to study the history of the Underground Railroad. In 2000, President Bill Clinton signed the National Underground Railroad Freedom Center Act. This act set aside $16 million to restore important historical sites and develop educational programs to teach people about this important part of American history. Today many of the Underground Railroad sites are museums.

People can still follow the routes and visit homes and other places that were part of the Railroad. One man named Anthony Cohen decided to trace the route that some slaves took to freedom. He started out in Maryland and walked 800 miles to Canada. On some days, he walked as many as 37 miles. He walked through the states of Maryland, Pennsylvania, and New York. It took him six weeks. Two years later, in 1998, he walked from Alabama to Canada, retracing another route of the "freedom train."

It took most escaped slaves much longer than that to reach freedom. Unlike Cohen, they could not walk in the daylight. They did not always have food, shelter, or warm clothing as he did. But they did not give up. By walking in their footsteps, Anthony honored the amazing strength and courage of those ordinary people who did extraordinary things to help one another be free. By remembering their stories and the struggles that they went through for freedom, the rest of us can honor them as well.

©Wayne Sorce

IN 1996, ANTHONY COHEN RETRACED A ROUTE ON THE
UNDERGROUND RAILROAD FROM MARYLAND TO CANADA.

©Wayne Sorce

HISTORIAN ANTHONY COHEN REJOICES AT THE END OF HIS 800-MILE JOURNEY.

Timeline

1619	Dutch slave traders land in Virginia, bringing the first African slaves to the United States.
1775	The first abolitionist group in the United States is founded in Philadelphia.
1798	Abolitionist Levi Coffin is born in North Carolina. As a child, he sees injustice against black people that will encourage him to fight slavery.
1826	Levi and Catharine Coffin move to Newport, Indiana, where they will live for more than 20 years. Their house becomes a station on the Underground Railroad, and they help more than 3,000 people escape slavery.
1838	Frederick Douglass runs away from slavery.
1847	Douglass publishes the first issue of the *North Star* newspaper, which provides information about the abolitionist movement.
1848	Ellen and William Craft escape to freedom, arriving in Pennsylvania on Christmas Day. They later move to Boston.
1849	Harriet Tubman escapes to freedom.
	Henry "Box" Brown packages himself in a box and is mailed to freedom.
1850	The Fugitive Slave Act is passed, providing for the return of runaway slaves to their owners. Anyone who helps slaves escape can be punished.
	Ellen and William Craft move to England to avoid being sent back to the South.

	Harriet Tubman makes her first trip back to the South to help other slaves escape to freedom on the Underground Railroad. Between 1850 and 1860, she helps more than 300 people to freedom, including her family.
1861	The American Civil War begins, with the North fighting the South.
1863	On January 1, President Abraham Lincoln signs the Emancipation Proclamation, stating that all slaves in the Confederate states are free.
1865	The Civil War ends. Slavery is abolished in the United States with the approval of the 13th Amendment to the U.S. Constitution.
1868	Ellen and William Craft return to the United States. They buy a farm and open a school for black children.
1990	The U.S. Congress asks the National Park Service to study the history of the Underground Railroad so that monuments can be identified and set aside.
1996	A historian named Anthony Cohen retraces an Underground Railroad route. He walks 800 miles from Maryland to Canada.
1998	Anthony Cohen again traces an Underground Railroad route, traveling from Alabama to Canada.
2000	President Bill Clinton signs the National Underground Railroad Freedom Center Act, setting aside $16 million to restore historic sites on the routes and create educational programs.

Glossary

abolitionists (ab-uh-LISH-uh-nists)
Abolitionists were people who worked to end (abolish) slavery before the American Civil War. Abolitionists believed that slavery was wrong and fought to change the laws that allowed it.

amendment (uh-MEND-ment)
An amendment is a change or addition made to the U.S. Constitution or other documents. The 13th Amendment to the Constitution ended slavery in the United States.

auction (AWK-shen)
An auction is a sale at which items are sold to the person who offers the most money. Slaves were sold at auctions.

bounty hunters (BOWN-tee HUN-terz)
Bounty hunters are people who earn reward money by catching fugitives. Bounty hunters tracked and captured escaped slaves.

Civil War (SIV-il WAR)
A civil war is a war between opposing groups of people within the same country. The U.S. Civil War was fought between the Northern and the Southern states from 1861 to 1865.

Confederate (kun-FED-er-et)
The Confederate states were the Southern states that left the Union in 1860 and 1861. The Confederate states wanted to maintain the practice of slavery.

Constitution (kon-stih-TOO-shun)
A constitution is the set of basic principles that govern a state, country, or society. Slavery was outlawed by an addition to the U.S. Constitution.

emancipation (ee-man-sih-PAY-shun)
Emancipation means setting something free. The Emancipation Proclamation was supposed to free slaves in the Confederate states.

enslaved (en-SLAYVD)
When people are enslaved, they are forced to be slaves or are owned by other people. People who are enslaved lose their freedom.

fugitive (FYOO-jih-tiv)
A fugitive is a person who is running away from something. The Fugitive Slave Act made it illegal to help slaves escape to freedom.

Glossary

oral history (OR-ul HIS-tuh-ree)
Oral history is a record of past events that is passed down by spoken word rather than in writing. Much of what is known about slave life has come from oral history.

overseer (OH-ver-see-er)
An overseer is a person who supervises others as they work. As a young girl, Harriet Tubman tried to protect another slave from an overseer.

surrender (suh-REN-dur)
If an army surrenders, it gives up to its enemy. Confederate General Robert E. Lee surrendered to the Union army in 1865.

Union (YOON-yen)
The Union is another name for the United States. During the Civil War, the term "Union" referred to the Northern states.

Index

Further Information

Books and Magazines

Blockson, Charles L. *The Underground Railroad: First Person Narratives of Escapes to Freedom in the North.* New York: Prentice Hall Press, 1987.

Cosner, Shaaron. *The Underground Railroad.* State College, PA: A Venture Book, 1991.

Freedman, Florence B., and Ezra Jack Keats (illustrator). *Two Tickets to Freedom: The True Story of Ellen and William Craft, Fugitive Slaves.* New York: Peter Bedrick Books, 1989.

Ringgold, Faith. *Aunt Harriet's Underground Railroad in the Sky.* New York, Crown Publishers, 1992.

Tobin, Jacqueline L., and Raymond G. Dobard. *Hidden in Plain View: A Secret Story of Quilts and the Underground Railroad.* New York: Doubleday, 1999.

Winter, Jeanette. *Follow the Drinking Gourd.* New York: Knopf, 1992.

Web Sites

Visit *National Geographic*'s Underground Railroad Site:
http://www.nationalgeographic.com/features/99/railroad/j1.html

Learn more about Anthony Cohen, who retraced Underground Railroad routes:
http://www.smithsonianmag.si.edu/smithsonian/issues96/oct96/undergroundrr.html
http://www.ugrr.org/walk98/index.htm

Visit a site on Harriet Tubman and the Underground Railroad (from Mrs. Taverna's second-grade class at Pocantico Hills School):
http://www2.lhric.org/pocantico/tubman/tubman.html

Visit the National Underground Railroad Freedom Center:
http://www.undergroundrailroad.com/

Visit the William Still Underground Railroad Foundation:
http://www.undergroundrr.com/indexfr.html

Learn Songs of the Underground Railroad:
http://www.appleseedrec.com/underground/